# Rothenburg

## on the Tauber

*Copperplate etching by Mathäus Merian (1648)*

# Guide to the most beautiful sights

We're always thankful for hints and suggestions to help us to keep this guide up to date.

# Rothenburg
## on the Tauber

**Kunstverlag Edm. v. König, Heidelberg/Dielheim**

Copyright 1998

Kunstverlag Edm. von König GmbH & Co. KG, Heidelberg/Dielheim.
Text by Wolfgang Kootz.
Photos: Fine art publishers Edm. von König
pp. 23, 28, 47 KL Fotostudios Galerie, Rothenburg
pp. 5, 33, 44 A. Cowin, Heidelberg
pp. 36, 37 by kind permission of the Imperial City's Museum
pp. 48, 49 by kind permission of the Doll and Toy Museum
pp. 50, 51, 52, 53 by kind permission of the Crime Museum
Map in pp. 92, 93 by kind permission of the Tourist Office,
Rothenburg on the Tauber

Orders:
Kunstverlag Edm. von König, Postfach 1027, 69232 Dielheim,
tel. 0 62 22/9 81 60

Further publications in this same series:
Berlin – Dinkelsbühl – Heidelberg – München – Nürnberg – Rhine Guide –
Schwäbisch Hall – Ulm an der Donau – Bodensee and Black Forest.

ISBN: 3-921934-09-5

*Total view of Rothenburg on the Tauber, a jewel from the Middle Ages.*

## A hearty welcome to Rothenburg

This once 'free imperial city' is known all over the world and ranks among Germany's most frequented towns. It lies on a plateau at the intersection of the so-called 'Romantic Route' 1,275 ft. above sea level. Below the town runs the River Tauber in its 180 ft deep valley and this is the reason why the town has the additional 'ob' or 'above' the Tauber. Most of its 12,500 inhabitants both inside and outside the city walls work to serve its many tourists. There are 19 hotels, 35 inns and boarding houses and numerous smaller, private concerns offering in all over 2000 beds. Ninety restaurants, wine taverns and cafés, all over them catering for the well-being and entertainment of their guests. As well as the great number of places worth visiting within the town itself, there are several walks through delightful countryside. For those who like sport, there are tennis courts, riding facilities, shooting, angling, bowling, a golf course and also the possibility to fly. There is also a swimming pool set in woodland and a neighbouring swimming pool.

# A short summary of the history of Rothenburg

10th cent.  The founding of a castle.

1108        The Earl of Rothenburg dies without issue and his line dies with him. Heinrich von Rothenburg gives the castle to the monastery at Comburg.

1116        Emperor Heinrich V bestows the settlement upon his nephew, Duke Konrad von Schwaben (Swabia) and so Rothenburg passes into the possession of the Hohenstaufen family.

1137        Konrad becomes king.

1141        The 'Hohen-Staufenburg Rothenburg' is built.

1152        Konrad dies. His nephew, Friedrich I "Barbarossa", becomes king, at this time "the child of Rothenburg", since he is only eight years of age.

1157        Friedrich, now 13, is knighted and becomes the new Duke of Rothenburg.

1167        Friedrich the "Fair", as he is now called, helps his cousin, Friedrich I, to drive the pope, Alexander III, from Rome and dies there of a fever. Rothenburg falls to Emperor Friedrich, who allows the town to be ruled by sheriffs.

12th cent.  The building of the first city walls begins. The Burgtor, Weißer Turm, Markusturm and Röderbogen are still intact today.

1265        A Dominican priory is founded.

1274        Rothenburg becomes a free imperial city under King Rudolf of Habsburg. The first extension of the city walls is undertaken to bring the newly settled residential area of tradesmen within its protective embrace.

1339        Rothenburg receives the right to form its own alliances from Emperor Ludwig the Bavarian.

1356        An earthquake destroys the entire fortifications, leaving only the "great house of the Duke", the Chapel of St. Blaise, which remain intact.

from 1300
onwards:    The building of St. Jakob's Church begun, completed 1510.

14th cent.  The second extension fo the city now encloses the Spital district within its walls.

ca. 1400    The city experiences its heyday with Toppler as powerful lord mayor and officer general of the cities of Ulm, Nördlingen, and Dinkelsbühl.

1407        War of the cities involves Rothenburg in a siege led by Count Friedrich von Nürnberg (Nuremberg) and the Bishop of Würzburg. Everything lying outside the city walls is razed to the ground and utterly destroyed.

1408        The Peace of Mergentheim brings tribulation to Rothenburg's citizens. Mayor Toppler is taken prisoner and left to die in a dungeon.

| | |
|---|---|
| 1505 | The eastern side of the Town Hall is completely destroyed by fire. |
| 1525 | The Peasants' War. Rothenburg allies itself to the peasants' leader, Florian Geyer. After defeat suffered from a prince's army, Geyer's protagonists undergo a mass execution at the hands of Casimir von Ansbach. The holy mass is once more introduced. |
| 1544 | Introduction of the Protestant church service. |
| 1572 | The foundation stone is laid for the Renaissance building of the Town Hall, the most important building in the town. |

*Tilly, general of the imperial forces during the Thirty Years' War. The legend of the "Mighty Draught" came into being when he conquered the city in 1631.*

| | |
|---|---|
| 1618–48 | The Thirty Years' War. In 1618 the Protestant "Union" met in the city. In 1631 the town is besieged and taken by Tilly and then in 1634 and 1645 by Piccolomini and Turenne respectively. According to legend, Nusch's so-called "Master Drink" (Meistertrunk) saved the city from wholesale destruction. The effects of war reduce the city to a nonentity. |
| 1802 | Rothenburg becomes part of Bavaria. |
| 1905 | The town is connected to other parts of the region by railway. |
| 1945 | Rothenburg is partially destroyed by bombs. An American general hinders its total destruction. |
| after 1945 | The town is rebuilt in the old style. The destroyed fortifications are restored with the support of friends and well-wishers from all parts of the world. |

# A Walk Through the Town
## The Market Place (Marktplatz)

This square, surrounded by patricians' houses, has witnessed much that has taken place on the historical stage even from quite early times, events that have also determined Rothenburg's destiny. In the year 1474, Emperor Friedrich III, seated on a throne set in front of the 'Ratsherrntrinkstube' (the building with the clock), bestowed Holstein upon Christian, King of Denmark. And here, on the 30th June, 1525, Casimir, Earl of Ansbach, had 21 alleged instigators to riot publicly beheaded during the Peasants' War. The city's chronicle reports that on that occasion 'blood ran in rivulets down Schmiedgasse'. Here, too, on the 30th October, 1631, women and children fell on their knees to beg for mercy from General Tilly, enraged that the town had put up so much resistance. Just one year later, Gustav Adolf's army of Protestants quartered in the town. Today, the square is still the town's pulsing centre and it is from here that our journey through the town and its past begins.

It is not only on these occasions that one has opportunity to sit down prior to setting off through the town. The Town Hall's steps are positively inviting and it's nice to be able to take opportunity to look around at the coming and going, to rest one's feet from the ardours of unyielding concrete, here at the focus of the town's life.

*View from the Town Hall overlooking the Market Place*

# 'Ratsherrntrinkstube' or City Councillors' Tavern

This is in the Market Place and sports three sorts of clock on its Baroque gable as well as a bell tower jauntily set on its apex. The lowest of these clocks is the city's main timekeeper, constructed in 1683. Above this is a 'calendar clock', then the imperial eagle and finally a sun dial. At 11 a. m., midday, one o'clock ant at two o'clock and again at 9 p. m. and 10 p. m. there appear figures representing the principal parties in the

*The gable of the Ratsherrntrinkstube or City Councillors' Tavern. In the windows left and right of the clock, Tilly and Nusch respectively.*

*The Elector's Tankard dated 1616 and thought to be 'Welcoming Tankard' of the imperial city. The vessel, whose capacity is three and a quarter litres or nearly seven pints, is at the centre of the story of the "Mighty Draught" and can be seen in the Reichsstadtmuseum or Imperial City Museum.*

'Meistertrunk' or Drinking Feat which took place during the Thirty Years' War. The story goes that General Tilly, on 30th October, 1631, after encountering stiff resistance from its citizens was finally able to take the town. Accordingly, it was to be plundered and destroyed and its councillors executed. On the following day, the keeper of the wine cellar offers Tilly a 3¼ litre tankard of heavy Franconian wine as a toast to his arrival*. The general for his part is willing to grant the city a pardon provided one of the councillors can drink off this beverage in one go. Nusch, a former mayor, manages it in ten minutes and so saves the city.

*Town Hall. Nearest to us is the Renaissance building (16th century) and dovetailed to it, the Gothic section dating from the 13th century with its Baroque arcades below facing the square.*

## 2 The Town Hall (Rathaus, lit. 'House of Council')

The Market Place is truly dominated by the impressive Renaissance facade of the Rathaus with its Baroque arcade. Behind this we see the Gothic part of the building with its 60 metre (Approx. 120 ft) high gable. In the year 1240, the Gothic building was burned down only to be rebuilt ten years later, but not completed until the end of the 14th century. What it looked like then can be seen from a contemporary painting on the back of the 'Zwolfbotenalter' or Altar of the Twelve Apostles in the church of St. Jakob. Once more, the front part of the building fell victim to fire in 1501. In the six years between 1572 and 1578 and under the direction of the Rothenburg stonemason and sculptor, Leonhard Weidmann, this magnificent Renaissance building was then erected and incorporated into what was left of the rest of the Gothic building, so that today we see an amalgam of the two. The arcade was placed there somewhat later in 1681. Those responsible for the building well knew how to harmoniously combine three different architectural styles.

## The Town Hall's interior

The stairs within the tower lead us into the spacious dimensions of the foyer on the first floor spanned above by a ceiling of heavy beams. To the left and right of the tower's portal we can see the coats of arms of Rothenburg's noble families, names such as Nusch, von Staudt, Bezold and Winterbach. One of the paintings shows Rothenburg's most famous mayor and officer general of several imperial cities, Heinrich Toppler in knight's armour. A bronze plaque recalls the name of Gustav Adolf who lodged here shortly before his death in October 1632. If we now advance towards the doorway opposite us we will presently find ourselves in the Gothic 'Kaisersaal' or 'Imperial Room' which is well worth seeing. The window seats, balustrade, the representation of the Last Judgement as well as other reliefs in the structure of the building are all of them artistically sculptured from stone.

The arch over the staircase tower is decorated with splendid Gothic tracery. Grouped around the German imperial eagle are the coats of arms of the electors and those of the city. Also to be seen is the monogram of Weidner, the master builder. Going up into the top storey we can eventually get out onto the tower gallery and thereby gain a marvellous view of the town with its sea of red roofs and innumerable turrets, towers and fortifications.

Having descended again to the inner courtyard between the two buildings, we discover a fine Renaissance portal and this, too, is probably Weidmann's work. Up to the completion of the newer section of the Town Hall in 1578, this was the principal entrance to the building.

**Town Hall (Rathaus):**
Times of opening 8 a.m. to 6 p.m.

(i) **Town Hall Tower (Rathausturm)**
Times of opening 1st April to 31st October inclusive, open daily from 9–12.30 p.m. and again from 1 p.m. to 4 p.m.
In the winter from 1st November to 31st March only weekend and festival from midday to 3 p.m.

*Rathaus (Town Hall). The Imperial Room showing the relief The Last Judgement.*

*Entrance to the Rathaus (Town Hall) in Renaissance style. This was at one time the main entrance to the Gothic building.*

*The Master Builder's House (Baumeisterhaus) built 1596 by Weidmann. To the right next to it, Mayor Toppler's house (14th century).*

## The Master Builder's House

The Obere Schmidgasse (Upper Smithy's Lane) joins the Market Place at its south-east corner. The first three patrician's houses to meet the eye embody the building styles of various periods. The 'Gasthof zum Greifen' was once the residence of Mayor Toppler. The building was first erected towards the end of the 14th century and restored in the 17th. The next house towards the Marktplatz is the finest house in the town, namely the Master Builder's House (Baumeisterhaus) built in 1596 in the Renaissance style by Leonhard Weidner for the city's master builder.

The 'steps' of the gable are ornamented by 'S'-shaped dragons and particularly noticeable are the supporting figures at the windows of both upper storeys of men and women alternately representing the seven virtues and vices. Thus, in the lower row we see Compassion, Gluttony, Motherly Love and Treachery standing next to one another. It is also worth having a look at the delightfully picturesque inner courtyard which is exactly as it was and which today is a café. The next house in this row with its coat of arms and steplike gable was formerly an apothecary.

*The picturesque inner courtyard of the Master Architect's House. In warm weather it was used by the patricians as extension of the living quarters.*

The 'Schmiedgasse' is decorated by artistic cantilevers and floral decorations in front of shops and inns.

## The Herterichs Well

In the south-west corner of the Marktplatz is the Herterichs Well, sometimes referred to as a fountain and also called St. George's Well. This well already supplied the city's needs in 1446. It acquired its present decorated, twelve-sided form from the hands of the Rothenburg mason, Christoph Körner, who re-styled the old well to this Renaissance one in 1608. The central column with its coats of arms is crowned by a statue of St. George. In the Middle Ages, the instruments of the city's powers of jurisdiction were set up here in front of the well, among them the gallows, the pillory and hoisted cage. Once a year, the shepherds danced around the well and so drove away the ever-present threat of plague. A legend tells of rejoicing shepherds dancing here over treasure which one of them had discovered in a dream. This traditional dance is performed several times a year in front of the Town Hall (see Calender of Events).

Next to the well is a half-timbered house, the Jagstheimer House and today the Marien Apotheke or chemist's shop, built for Lord Mayor Jagstheimer of this city in 1488. The projecting bay at its corner has a figure of the Virgin Mary beneath it. The picturesque courtyard, so peacefully reminiscent of days past, with its richly ornamented galleries or balconies is a magnificent example of a wealthy burgher's courtyard about this time.

*Herterichsbrunnen or Herterichs Well with its St. George's figure and for that reason sometimes called St. George's Well. To the left, Jagstheimer House and on the right the Town Hall.*

## 3 Art exhibition in the 'Meat and Dance House' (Fleisch- und Tanzhaus)

The half-timbered house with the high gable behind the well stands on the foundations of the former town hall, destroyed in 1240. On the first floor right up until the 18th century, butchers used to sell their meat and sausages here, hence its name: das Fleisch- und Tanzhaus – the Meat and Dance House. Today, it houses exhibitions of work by the many artists who live in and around the town. The works exhibited are for the most part purchasable. The latter part of the house name is derived from the fact that at one time festive occasions were celebrated in the large room above the arches.

*The Imperial City's "Meat and Dance House" showing Herterichs Well and to the right Jagstheimer House and the Town Hall's bay window.*

**Art exhibitions:**

Fleisch- und Tanzhaus am Marktplatz. Times of opening from 1st April to 31st October, open daily from 10 a.m. to 5 p.m. also during 'Wintermärchen'. Entry free.

# 4 Historical Vaults and dungeons

Diagonally opposite to the Meat and Dance House lies the entrance to the patio and the Historical Vaults. Here you can have a look at an exposition of objects and scenes from the Thirty Year's War, as well as at utensils from the historical festival 'Der Meistertrunk'. Within these arches at one time odds-and-ends shops were to be found whose function it was to sell off those few wares not sold by the artisans themselves.

Accompanied by the caretaker of the building (janitor), we can descend two flights below the Emperor's Room and so come to the dungeon and next to it an old torture chamber. Here, there are three, narrow, dark rooms and it was here that Heinrich Toppler, mayor of the city, his eldest son, Jakob, and a cousin were held prisoner in the year 1408. Toppler himself died after two months on the 13th June of that year. It is not certain, whether he was murdered or not, but in the next month, following petitions for their release, his two relatives were set free.

*Historical vaults: Soldiers at dice, a scene from the Thirty Years' War.*

(i) **Historiengewölbe:**
Entrance at the Rathaus, Lichthof. Times of opening from Easter to 31st October 10 a.m. to 5 p.m. In April and October from 9 a.m. to 5 p.m. Closed at March at November.

We leave the patio at its other end and approach St. Jakobus Church. In front ot it we turn right.

## 5 The Old Grammar School (Altes Gymnasium)

The fine Renaissance building with the eight-sided tower to the north side of Church Square (Kirchplatz) is the former high or grammar school built in 1589. Today, it is used by the church as a community centre.

*The Old Grammar School or High School (Altes Gymnasium 1589) with its staired tower.*

*Romantic view of St. Jakobskirche.* ►

## 6 St. Jakobus' Church (Jakobskirche)

Now we will take a look at the main church of Rothenburg. More than a hundred years of work elapsed on this, Rothenburg's main church, before it was finally consecrated in the year 1448. Built in the high Gothic style with open tower tops, its massive form dominates Rothenburg's skyline.

A closer look allows us to appreciate the details of Gothic building. It is typical in that it has slim windows; its tall pillars and steeples all emphasize one another in striving upwards in aspiration towards God. This, Rothenburg's parish church, was first erected by the Knights of the

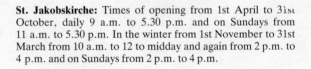

**St. Jakobskirche:** Times of opening from 1st April to 31st October, daily 9 a.m. to 5.30 p.m. and on Sundays from 11 a.m. to 5.30 p.m. In the winter from 1st November to 31st March from 10 a.m. to 12 to midday and again from 2 p.m. to 4 p.m. and on Sundays from 2 p.m. to 4 p.m.

German Order on the site of a former parish church and sister church to that in the older settlement of Detwang. The money for its erection however was put up by the citizens of Rothenburg and because of its long drawn-out time of building, there were naturally quite a number of architects and planners involved in its construction. Legend has it that when the towers were constructed, the south tower was built by the master himself and the more slender north tower by his apprentice. As it happened, the latter was a better piece of work than that put up by the master and in a fit of anger he threw himself from the tower and was killed.

Entry to the church is through the south porch and as we do so we catch sight of the richly-decorated 'Bridal Door' to our right. If we have found the exterior of the church impressive enough, the inside now offers us if anything an even more impressive scene. There are a number of out-standing examples of German Gothic artistry, all of whose enormous creative energy is dedicated to exclusively decorating this place of worship. On looking around for a moment, we see that pointed arcades combine the high central nave with the lower aisles, while above them the walls are light and unadorned, having slim pillars only which lead over to what is called crossvaulting.

*St. Jakob's Church showing the richly–decorated bridal porch on its south side.*

*St. Jakob's Church, Rothenburg's principal church in the high Gothic style, built in the 14th and 15th centuries and having different tops to its towers.*

## The church's interior works of art

In the south aisle below the gallery we find a depiction of the prophet Elias. Moving now in the direction of the choir, we come across the back of a former altar, pass a memorial tablet and, at the opening to the Spörlein Chapel, a figure of the Virgin Mary. The chapel which then follows is dedicated to Rothenburg's famous lord mayor, Heinrich Topp-ler (d. 1408) who left many noteworthy endowments to this church. Moving along again, we pass a statue of St. Jacobus and the Hornburg

*St. Jakobs Kirche (St. James's Church) showing the nave and choir, the Altar of the Twelve Apostles and its colourful, medieval windows.*

*Jakobskirche (St. James's Church) showing the Altar of the Twelve Apostles its shrine and carved figures. The altar wings and the predella show paintings by Friedrich Herlin (ca. 1430–1500).*

epithaph and at the end of this side aisle we stand before the altar of the Crowning of the Virgin Mary. This work of art came into being about 1520, but it is not certain whose work it is; it is assumed to be that of the Riemenschneider School. The crowning of the Virgin adorns the shrine itself and below, in the predella, Mary's death, on the wings of the altar, St. Anne, the Virgin with child and Christ himself. This was a frequent combination of figures during the late Middle Ages.

Four remarkable sculptures, those of St. Christopher, St. George, John the Baptist and St. John the Divine ornament the first column, and passing into the raised area of the choir which was built between 1311 and 1322, we find ourselves in the oldest part of the church. The figure of St. Peter greets us at the level of the steps. The choir stalls were erected by a Rothenburg master in 1514 for member Knights of the German Order. Above them hang paintings of former principal preachers in this church after the Reformation. The altar is the dominating subject in this part of the church, the wonderful altar of the Twelve Apostles. It is one of the most important historic treasures in Germany, and came into being in 1466, financed by a generous gift on the part of Mayor Toppler and his wife. The magnificent sculptures are the work of Swabian masters, the most impressive perhaps being the crucifix as central figure surrounded

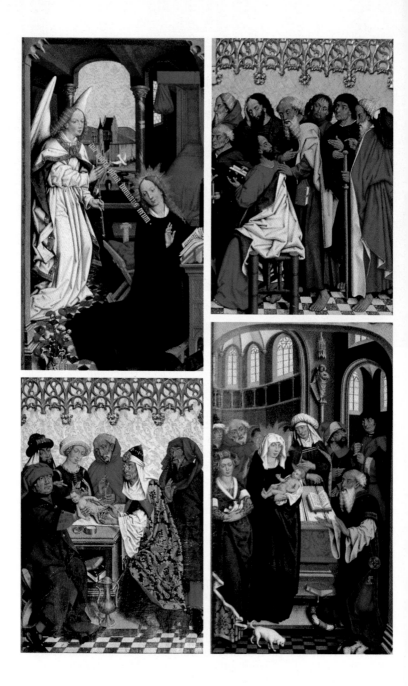

*Sections of the painting panels by Friedrich Herlin.*

by four angels. Among the figures we can recognise the Virgin Mary, St. Jacobus, the patron of the church and St. Elizabeth; to the right stands St. John, St. Leonard and St. Anthony. The scene at the bottom shows Jesus in the company of his disciples and it is this which gave the altar its name.

The paintings all stem from workshop of Friedrich Herlin who worked in Nördlingen for the most part. On the inner sides of the altar wings are scenes from the life of the Virgin Mary: to the left there is the Annunciation and the Visitation of the Blessed Virgin Mary, the Birth of Christ and the Circumcision and to the right the Worship of the Three Kings, Christ in the Temple and, on two of the pieces, Mary's death. The tablets at the extremes show the death and the legends associated with the life of St. Jacobus. When the altar wings are closed, the sequence of presentations is as follows:

1. Preaching and his being taken prisoner. 2. Execution. 3. Transportation of the body into a medieval town after which follow scenes from the legend of St. Jacobus: 4. Pilgrims on their way to St. Jacobus' grave. The wicked landlord slyly packing a golden beaker into a travelling bag. 5. The landlord accuses the pilgrims of stealing. The beaker is found and the son of the pilgrim sacrifies himself and is hanged. 6. The father finds his son whom the holy Jacobus has preserved alive on the gallows. Together with the judge he returns to the inn. 7. The landlord declares that the son is as dead as the chickens on his spit. These then fly away. The judge leads the wicked landlord away to the gallows. The young

*The Altar of the Twelve Apostles. On it one can see Rothenburg's Town Hall (Rathaus) as it was in the 15th century.*

pilgrim is taken down from the gallows and accompanies his father homewards. Of particular interest is the city scene depicting the despatch of St. Jacobus' body. It is one of the oldest true-to-life representations of a German city and shows Rothenburg's town hall and market place as they looked before the great fire of 1501.

*St. Jacob's church: Richly appointed niche for the sacraments, built in 1377.*

To the east in the choir area and forming an end to it are three valuable stained-glass window paintings some 46 ft. high which come into their own during the morning when they throw their wonderful colours into the interior of the church. The central window, which dates from the year 1350, shows scenes from the life and passion of Christ surrounded by the prophets. The windows to right and left (both produced around 1400) show Christ's work of redemption and the life of the Blessed Virgin.

Above the northern row of the choir stalls we can see the coats of arms of noble Rothenburg families who looked after the interests of the church during their lifetime and who here receive acknowledgement. The statue of St. Michal bids us farewell at the steps of the choir.

On the left adjacent to the high altar a large and richly appointed niche for the sacraments is built into the side wall of the choir. This work of art with its many figures revolves around the theme of the Eucharist and the sacraments of the altar, while the representation of the Trinity in the form of the so-called Mercy Seat above the actual niche (for storing the liturgical vessels) is the focus of attention. This very significant sculptural work was built in approx. 1377 and it has unfortunately not been fully preserved in its present form.

The first pillar in the nave of the church is decorated by four apostolic figures; the next one which supports the pulpit was installed in 1854. On the outer wall each at the same height, there are three epitaphs to be seen set in the wall itself showing a bishop and an impressive depiction of Our Lord of Sorrows flanked by the Wörnitzer and Häuptlein Chapels. The third column is ornamented by the figures of St. Mathew and St. Eustachius.

The new organ was installed in 1968 above the west gallery and has been praised by specialists all over the world for its superb fullness of tone and the splendid definition of its individual stops. It has two consoles and altogether six keyboards, 69 registers and 5500 pipes. Those interested in organ music should not miss attending a recital.

## The Holy Blood Altar

We can go up the steps to the west choir and allow the most precious work of art the church has to offer simply have its effect on us. Again, this is the work of the distinguished artist, Riemenschneider, who lived from 1460 to 1531. This, the Holy Blood Altar, was carved and set up

*The Altar of the Holy Blood, one of Riemenschneider's masterpieces. The imposing superstructure of the altar contains a gold-plated cross holding holy relics.*                                                                              ▶

between the years 1499 and 1505 and commissioned by the Rothenburg Town Council so as to provide an honourable respository for a relic of Holy Blood. According to legend, it is said that 3 drops of Christ's blood is contained within a capsule of rock crystal in the gold-plated cross (1270) and this is what has given the altar its name. The beautiful altar as a whole was assembled in the workshop of the Rothenburg master, Erhard Harschner. The wonderfully presented scene of the Last Supper here exquisitely carved from limewood is unmistakably the artistry of Riemenschneider. The central figure is that of Judas which is unusual seen here standing alone with the money bag while Christ in offering a portion of bread to him says: 'One of you shall betray me'. The disciples, each according to his temperament, react with dismay, astonishment or fall to discussion as to whom it may be. Only John remains unperturbed and confident in the presence of his Lord. Both the finely carved altar wings to left and right and the open lattice work to the rear of the composition heighten the effect of this masterpiece on the beholder. The altar wings display scenes of Christ's entry into Jerusalem and the agony of Gethsemane showing the sleeping disciples in the foreground and Christ praying in the middle. In the background we can see the approach of those with sticks and staves with Judas at their head.

*The Altar of the Holy Blood. Its principal picture is that of the Last Supper showing Judas in the middle and Christ offering him the bread.*

*The Altar of the Holy Blood showing James the Less.*

*The Altar of the Holy Blood showing John the disciple sleeping.*

*The Holy Blood Altar: Scenes of the Lord's Last Supper.*

*The so-called 'Feuerleinserker' with St. Jakob's Church in the background.*

We leave the main church and turn right into the 'Klingengasse' which passes below the choir of the church. There we find a delightfully picturesque window bay set at the corner of a half-timbered house and, at the rear, Jakobskirche. This, too, is one of Rothenburg's prettiest views.

*Popular 'means of transport' in Rothenburg.*

# 7 The Imperial City's Museum (Reichsstadtmuseum) to be found in the Dominican Priory

Proceeding along Klingengasse, we presently come to a side lane leading towards the priory courtyard which is dominated by a very large yellow building, and we find ourselves standing in front of the former Dominican priory which, together with St. Jakob's church and the Town Hall, belongs to Rothenburg's most notable historic buildings.

The priory was founded as an endowment from the Master of the Imperial Kitchens, Lupold von Nordenberg, in 1258. The wealthy dowries of the ladies living here, most of them the daughters of the local well-to-do, enabled the building to be considerably extended and modified during the course of several centuries up to its dissolution as a result of the Reformation in 1544. Under Bavarian administration, too, right up to the year 1806, this complex of buildings underwent various changes. Since 1936, its living quarters, dormitories, its workrooms with their large beams dating from the 14th century, its kitchen which dates from about 1300, its convent room and summer refectory added in the 15th and 16th centuries respectively, the winter refectory with its 15th century wooden barrel-vaulting, its hall for secular activities with its coloured ceiling, completed between 1725 and 1732, a collection of Rothenburg works of art and culture, all these today provide a roof for exhibitions of

*Oldest kitchen to be seen in the Dominican Priory here showing the vast chimney above the cooking range and hearth.*

*Early Baroque period cupboard made of at least 7 different species of wood.*

*29 The partially gold-plated silver cup of the Rothenburg Retailers' Association, produced in Nuremberg in the year 1687.*

furniture, paintings, sculptures, arms, household ware, workmen's tools and farming equipment. Among the most important exhibits is the work of Martinus Schwarz, the so-called 'Rothenburg Passion', a cycle of twelve paintings depicting scenes from Christ's passion dated 1494. In addition to this, the original, glazed 'Elector's Tankard' (1616) can be seen around which the story of the 'Meistertrunk' is woven.

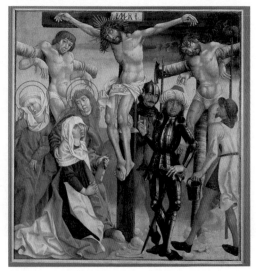

*Scene from the Rothenburg Passion Cycle (1494) showing the Crucifixion.*

In the gallery here one can also view the works of the English painter, Arthur Wasse (1854–1930) whose paintings have managed to capture the many moods of the city in a peculiarly romantic way.

*Arthur Wasse (1854–1930):*
*View upon St. James Church from the north side. Painted in oil on linen.*

**The imperial City's Museum** (Reichsstadtmuseum):

ⓘ Times of opening: 1st April to 31st October, open daily from 9 a.m. to 5 p.m. other month 10 a.m. to 12 midday and again from 2 p.m. to 4 p.m.

## 8 Klingen Gate (Klingentor)

We leave the Imperial City's Museum and walk along the Klingengasse in northern direction to the Klingen Gate. This gate tower with its corner turrets is over 30 metres (82 ft.) high. Like the other towers of the city's ramparts, the Prison Tower, Gallows Tower, Röder Tower and Kobolzeller Gate, it, too, was built towards the end of the 14th century. In the 16th century, a copper water trap was installed in it to act as a reservoir for the several wells of the town, one of which, for example, was Herrnbrunnen. To reinforce the city's defences even more, a further bastion was erected around 1500 in front of this tower, even St. Wolfgang's church being enlisted to defend the city and instead of church windows, the wall to the outside has loopholes and defensive positions behind its massive stonework. Additional protection was afforded by a drawbridge placed in front of the outer tower. The town augmented the fortifications between church and gate by means of a moveable rampart equipped with pieces of artillery and this can be seen together with the other town defences and the church.

*Working equipment from the Museum of Rural Life.*

 **Museum of Rural Life:** Klingengasse
Opening times: Easter–31st October 10 a.m. to 5 p.m.

*St. Wolfgang's church or Shepherds' Church, a fortified 15th century church whose outer wall in fact belongs to the outer ramparts of the city.*

## St. Wolfgang's Church or Shepherd's Church

This late Gothic church was erected after 1475 on the spot where shepherds prayed and for that reason is called 'Schäfer-Kirche' or Shepherds' Church. St. Wolfgang, on the other hand, was the patron saint of their guild who protected their wandering herds from the jaws of the wolf. One can see him depicted on a relief between the church doors below the crucifix.

The high altar shows St. Wolfgang, flanked by St. Sebastian and St. Rochus and on the altar wings there are pictures showing scenes from the lives of the three saints. St. Wendelin's altar and that of the Holy Virgin, together with the magnificent vaulted roof all contribute to the splendour of the church's interior. The paintings on the altar wings of the high altar and that of the altar to the Virgin Mary are the work of the Rothenburg painter, Wilhelm Ziegler and date from 1514–15.

Stone steps in the massive north wall near the high altar lead to the vaulted defensive positions below the church and referred to above. The spiral staircase in the opposite corner is that which leads to the gate tower and its observation post and to the sentry walk in the north wall.

*St. Wolfgang's Church. The vaulting, which goes back to the late Gothic period, spans the interior with its three altars.*

Through a side door we reach the area of the former castles, today called Castle Gardens.

 **St. Wolfgang's Church:**
(Pfarrkirche): Open from 1st April to 31st October from 10 a.m. to 1 p.m. and again from 2 p.m. to 5 p.m. Rest of time closed.

*Rothenburg's Burgtor or Castle Gate (14th century) at night. This is the city's largest and oldest tower here showing the first gate, guardhouse and customs house.*

# 9  Castle Gate (Burgtor)

The Castle Gate is the mightiest and oldest of Rothenburg's gates (12th century). At one time a drawbridge spanned the moat between the gate-house and its outer ramparts. The first gate with its coats of arms, its guardhouse and little customs house were in fact added after 1590.

# 10 Castle Gardens (Burggarten)

These once formidable battlements have now become transformed into a park with a splendid view over the Tauber Valley. It was here that Rothenburg originated and here that the Franconian castle was erected by the dukes of Rothenburg probably in the 10th century. When their line died out, the Hohenstaufen family extended the castle's precincts. Under this patronage a thriving community grew up in the 12th to the 14th centuries as a result of the settlement of craftsmen and servants. At the beginning of the 15th century it had a total population of some 20,000 inhabitants. From the castle's terrace we have a marvellous view over the Tauber Valley with its numerous mills, many of them still in good working order, and of the ancient village of Detwang.

*Flowering splendour to be seen in Burggarten.*

The hill opposite is called Engelsberg or Angel's Hill because 200 years ago when the Celts inhabited the area, they built an earthwork fort to which they could retire when pursued. From its bare top one can probably gain the best all-round view of this medieval city and it was from there that Merian, distinguished for his etchings (1593–1650), made a drawing of the town. To our left we can see the western ramparts of the town as far as Klingentor and to the right as far as Stöberleinsturm in the so-called 'Kappenzipfel'.

## Blasius Chapel (Blasiuskapelle)

Only one building of the imperial castle survived to some extent the earthquake, probably the Palas. About 1400, the mayor Toppler gave the order to rebuild the ruin and to decorate the inside with mural paintings. The building which is also called the 'House of Dukes' serves today as a memorial place for the dead soldiers of both world wars.

The last witnesses of the castle architecture in a High Romanesque style from the period of the Hohenstaufen Emperers are the voluminous square stones. The citizens of Rothenburg used the remains of the other buildings for the construction of their houses and of the citywall.

*The massive Strafturm on the northwest flank of the city walls.*

## Herrngasse (Gentry Lane)

Through the Castle Gate we return into the city. The first building on the left side is the famous Puppet Theatre Trexler's figure theatre for adults.

(i) **Puppet Theatre:**
Times of opening 1st April to 31st October daily 8.30 p.m.
From June to September at 3 p.m. and again at 8.30 p.m. except Sundays.

The Herrengasse, lined by proud patricians' houses, is the connection between the Castle Gardens and the Town Hall. It's also called 'Herrenmarkt' (Gentry Market) because there used to be a horse and cattle market, a privilege of the patrician.

There is not one gable like another and above each attic hatch there is a projecting beam used to facilitate the hoisting of loads for storage in the loft. At times of emergency and in war, every household was required to store a specified quantity of foodstuffs and other essential commodities. Inscriptions and plaques bear witness to the fact that emperors and kings have lodged for a night in these venerable old houses.

*Picturesque draw well to found in the courtyard of a wealthy citizen's hous*

*Herrngasse (Gentry Lane) shows wealthy burghers' houses lining Rothenburg's widest avenue. In the foreground we see the Herrnbrunnen and at the end, the Town Hall's tower.*

The 'Herrenbrunnen' in the middle of this street was set up in 1595. The town was obliged to bore several wells within the city because of its elevated position above the Tauber. The actual position of the outlying conduits were kept carefully secret and known only to the mayor and council. This was important since in time of war or siege the enemy could stop up the supply or poison the source.

Houses No. 11 and 15 have retained their romantic inner courts in the same way as the house opposite with its finely-wrought ironwork in front of the windows. This house once sheltered Emperors Charles V and Ferdinand I as well as the Queen of Sweden and the wife of Gustav Adolf (Gustavus Adolphus). The charming courtyard with its balconies, oriel window and winding staircase tower is probably the most delightful in all Rothenburg.

Inside this distinctive house we discover a large wooden staircase leading up to the first floor. The house is still lived in by the von Staudt family and ancestral portraits are testimony of a four hundred year-long tradition.

(i) **Staudtscher Patrizierhof:**
Times of opening from 1st April to 31st October from 9.30 a.m. to 5 p.m. From 1st November till 31st March closed.

*The romantic courtyard of the house belonging to the noble family of Staudt with its several galleries*

## 12 Franciscan Church

The high gothic Franciscan Church in the middle of the Herrngasse (Lords' Lane) belonged to an adjacent monastery of mendicant friars founded in 1281. The unpretentious basilica was consecrated in 1309. Inside, a wooden gallery, 'Lettner' or rostrum divides the choir into two and was once the place where the monks sat, the nave of the church being reserved for the congregation. The pictures, now partially obliterated, show the stations of the cross and go back to the 14th century. In the floor of the church and on its walls we discover numerous tombstone engravings as well as the bronze coats of arms of various noble Rothenburg families and those of neighbouring aristocracy. Dietrich von Berlichingen, the grandfather of the famous Götz von Berlichingen is buried here. The tablet to the memory of Hans von Beulendorf and his spouse, Margreth, on the northern pillar near the choir gallery is worth having a look at.

Furthermore, the ornate Franciscan altar depicting the stigmatization of Saint Francis of Assisi – one of Riemenschneider's works – is also erected in the church. The adjacent monastery building now houses Rothenburg's Goethe Institute in which foreigners today can learn German.

*The Church of St. Francis showing Herrnbrunnen (Gentry Well) in the foreground.*

*The interior of the Church of St. Francis.*

# 13 The Doll and Toy Museum (Puppen- und Spielzeug Museum)

The picturesque Hofbronnengasse leads to the Doll and Toy Museum near the Herterich's Well. Close to the market, only some steps behind the St. George's Well, the Hofbronnengasse begins, where on the right hand, rather hidden, lies the Hofbronnen, a well the lane got its name from.

In the second house of the 'Hofbronnengasse', the no. 13, you find one of the most beautiful toy museums in Germany. It is worthwhile taking the time to turn one's mind back to the dreamworld of the childhood.

In this house from the 15th century, classified as a historical monument, a private doll and toy museum was opened in 1984. 200 years of history of toys and more than 600 dolls from manufactures in Germany, France and other European countries are tenderly exposed with the appropriate accessories in playful scenes.

*'We play with the model railway'*
*Model railway from 1900 made by Rock & Graner, Biberach.*

 **Doll Museum:**
Hofbronnengasse. Times of opening daily 9.30 a.m. to 6 p.m. In the winter from 1th January to 28th February from 11 a.m. to 5 p.m.

Lovely doll's houses and toy shops show the way of living of our ancestors. But also tin toys, model trains, theatres, farms a circus, merry-go-rounds, the bustle of a fair and handmade wooden toys as well as thousends of lovely toys of a longly passed childhood come back to life.

In the wintertime from the end of November to the end of February there is another remarkable exposition. In the 400-year old vault cave of the toy museum more than 20 Christmas cribs and many other subjects showing the godliness of the people are exposed.

Only godlings a few meters down into the valley the Crime Museum is situated.

*Doll's House from about 1900 Handmade model furniture, carved and decorated by marquetry.*

*Characteristic doll from Kämmer & Reinhardt Series no. 114 with dog 'Bully' made by Steiff.*

*One of the most beautiful colored dolls made by Simon & Halbig Series no. 1358, sitting characteristic doll made by Robert Maaser.*

*Instruments for torture and punishment in the basement.*

*Ducking cage for bakers who sold too small loaves baker's.*

It is the only one museum of law in the european area, beside this it is the most important collection of the history of rights there is. In 4 floors, about 2000 square-meters, and in more than 130 glass-cases the museum gives you a unique and complete glance at more than on thousand years of history of law. Shown is the development of jurisprudence to the 19th century. In addition to state and constitutional law, a prime interest to us concerns civil degradation penalties and police laws, which are very revealing with respect to the notions, laws, customs and cultures of our forefathers. Additionally, these exhibits include instruments of torture, items used in the execution of sentences, costly books, graphic arts, documents of emperors, princes, the nobility and towns. Also included are coats of arms, seals, crafts, trades and patents of the nobiltiy: caricatures of the judiciary, juristic ex libris, schools and their punishments, law and justice in the medal, and the legal symbolisms from seven centuries. By coming to Rothenburg, you will discover a medieval town with strong walls, buildings of Gothic and Renaissance style, churches, and Patrician houses. All these are testimony of the past life of an old imperial city and its citizens. However, while touring our town, you will probably find these show a very limited aspect of medieval life and for this reason ask yourself many questions. Buildings alone are not the answer of these questions. For this reason it is our opinion that you do not get to know a medieval town without hearing or seeing something specific about it. A visit to the town cannot be complete without visiting The Medieval Crime Museum.

*Part of view of the exhibition room.*

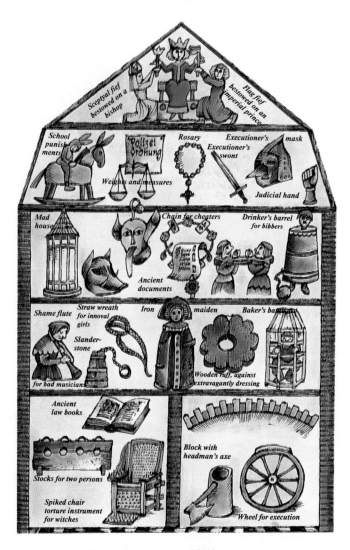

*Explications to the illustrations on page 52/53.*

1. Wooden ruff, for women who violated clothing regulations.
2. Mask of shame for women. The long tongue and big ears symbolize gossip and nosiness.
3. Mask of shame with long snout.
4. Drunk barrel for bibbers.
5. Mask of shame for men who acted like a swine.
6. Double-neck-violin, for two quarrelsome women.
7. Stock, for men on pane of being exposed publicly.
8. Iron maiden a mantle of infamy for women and girls, 16th century.
9. Mask of shame for men.
10. Donkey of shame, for lazy pupils.
11. Spiked-chair, an instrument of torture from the witch trial era.
12. Neck-violin, degrading punishment for women and girls.
13. Shame-flute for bad musicians.

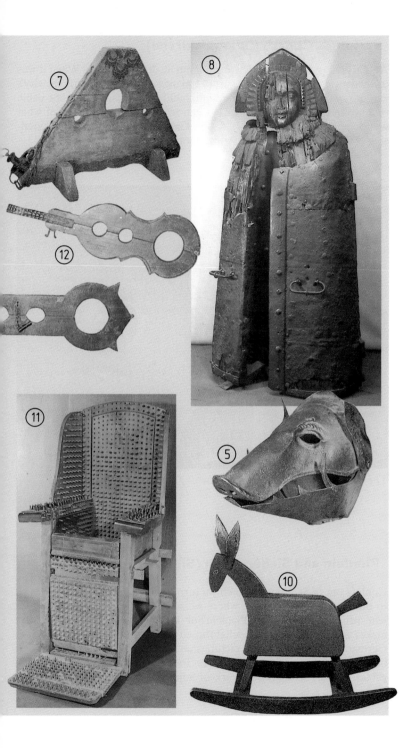

## 15 St. John's Church (Johanniskirche)

At this point we are only a few yards from St. John's Church. When it was erected around the year 1400, part of the masonry once forming the city's earlier ramparts was incorporated into building this church. On the gable side of the church, for example, we can still see the gate hinges of what was once the city gate, the 'St. John's Gate' which, after the first extension of the city, simply became superfluous.

*The sign of a hotel in the Schmiedgasse.*

## 16 Plönlein and Siebersturm (Sieber's Tower)

Coming out of St. John's Church we turn right and walk some steps back to the Untere Schmiedgasse where we soon stand on the famous 'Plönlein' originally known as 'Plänlein' or Little Square. This intersection makes up one of the must delightful city views obtainable anywhere in Germany. Before us lies the picturesque, halftimbered house with a well in front of it framed by the Siebers Tower and Kobolzeller Gate. The gables and the wrought ironwork of adjoining guesthouses enhance the charm of the scene.

*Siebersturm (13th century) seen from the Spital quarter. It served as the southern defence of the city before its second extension.*

The Sieber's Tower in the 'Spitalgasse' is protected on its outside by huge square stones. In the 12th century, the Gate of the Order of St. John formed the southern entrance to the city. However, as more and more tradesmen began to settle in the outskirts of the city as a result of its growing prosperity, measures were taken as early as 1204 to accomodate the new residential areas within the protective confines of the city walls.

*Plönlein and Siebersturm.* ▶

## 17 Kobolzeller Gate or Tower

The defences of the gate ensured protection of the road up from the Tauber Valley, the so-called "Steige" or incline. Passing through the gate we find ourselves in the four-cornered bastion with its crenelated 'Devil's Pulpit' which functioned as a lookout. The gate whose outside wall is decorated with the coats of arms of the imperial city is defensively overlooked by the adjoining tower, the Kohlturm.

Because of the sloping ground just in front of the gate, the building constructors of those times did not venture to place the tower over the gate as was general practice. If we go a little way down the slope we have a superb view of this gate and its defences with the Siebersturm in the background.

*Kobolzeller Gate or Tower. On its outer wall one can see the coats of arms of the imperial city (the imperial eagle) and the coats of arms of the city itself. To the left, the 'Devil's Pulpit' and in the background the Siebersturm.*

*The inner court of the Kobolzeller Gate.*

## 8  Roßmühle (Nag's Mill)

The path above the bastion leads us to the Nag's Mill, a compact building supported by flying buttress. If, in time of war or drought, the supply of flour ran out in the Tauber Valley, sixteen horses would be harnessed here to grind the corn.

To the rear of the building which is a youth hostel today we find the rest of what was once a large lime tree which was known to be flourishing in 1587.

*Roßmühle (Nag's Mill) formerly having four grinding wheels and driven by sixteen horses. Today, it is a youth hostel.*

## 9  The 'Hegereiterhaus' and the 'Spitalhof'

Our walk leads us on to the infirmary courtyard which is dominated by the unique character of the Hegereiter House in the middle. Its pointed tent roof and round tower topped by a decorative, lantern-like turret, provides a charming contrast to the sober, functional buildings surrounding it. This building, too, along with the main building is the work of Weidmann. A large kitchen is housed on the ground floor while the upper storey is used for living in and at one time provided an appartment for the horse trainer of the various Spital estates. In the main building, that is the part which has a gable and looks on to the street, the Spital administra-

*The Hegereiterhaus.*

tive offices were once housed and later, up to 1948, it served as a hospital proper. Today, it is an old people's home. There is a well to be found behind beautiful wrought-iron work on the north side of the building in the cellar and bakery which is a young hostel today.

*The peace of evening on the Spital battlements.*

## The Stöberleinsturm

In comparison, the legendary Stöberleinsturm seems almost toy-like with its quaint corner bay windows. The Spital district 'of the Holy Ghost' as it was called, came into being about 1280 when, as was customary at that time for every medieval town, the infirmary was built outside the city precincts. A number of endowments at its inauguration and numerous gifts of money in the centuries following enabled the members of the Order to care for its sick and its poor. Along with this, they administrated the Spital's estates and up until this area was taken within the city walls also accommodated travellers with a night's lodging who were no longer allowed into the city after dark.

*The legendary Stöberlein Tower (Stöberleinsturm).*

## The Spitalkirche or Hospital Church

The foundation stone of the Gothic Spitalkirche was already laid in 1281. The valuable figures making up the altar scene which was erected here in 1953 go back to the first half of the 15th century. They consist of a crucifix of wood flanked by stone effigies of St. John and the Virgin Mary. One of the tombstone nameplates recalls that of Count Otto von Flügelau (d. 1317), one of the donors towards the church's erection. The statue of the Virgin Mary to the right of the choir also stems from this

*Spitalkirche (1281). To the right of the altar the pulpit and to the left the front and the tabernacle.*

period. The sacraments cabinet opposite (ca. 1390) depicts on its right and left scenes from the Annunciation which include the angel Gabriel. Above the door one sees the Christ child on a rainbow, here to be understood as a bridge between man and God, whose end sweeps down to Our Lady. Above all, however, stands Christ. The niche served in earlier times to hold the wine and host used at mass.

*The Hospital Quarter (Spital-viertel). Behind the formidable battlements of the Spital, we can see the extensive roof of the hospital itself.*

The sturdy building of the Zehntscheune (Zehnt Barn) forms the western end of the extensive Spital district and goes back to the year 1699. In 1975, European Monument Preservation Year, this building was transformed into a modern congress building, the Imperial City Festival Hall or Reichstadthalle. The hall can accommodate 150 to 500 people at one sitting and as many as 600 if they are to be seated in rows.

We leave the area of the Holy Ghost Hospital and walk into the direction of the southern Tower Gate.

*The Spital or so-called Hospital Bastion (16th cent.) with its seven gates, portcullis, drawbridge and moveable ramparts provided a most formidable bulwark to the town's defences.*

## 21 The Spital Bastion

This is the most recent addition to the town's defences and was added in the 16th century by Leonhard Weidmann. The two fortifications, placed behind one another so as to form an 'eight' and which were equipped with portcullis and drawbridge and an additional moveable barricade on which pieces of artillery were placed, made this bastion into one of the most formidable in the whole town. The inscription on the keystone of this grim bulwark reads: 'Pax intrantibus. Salus exeuntibus'. i. e. Peace to those who enter. Farewell to those who leave!

The ramparts have recently been restored to their original condition and can be viewed by the public. The 'Adventure Playground' for children in the city's moat bed offers both children and adults a welcome opportunity to rest after tramping on cobblestones through the city's history!

## The 'Faulturm'

Having left the Spital Bastion, we walk along the city walls in northern direction, and then we stand in front of the huge 'Faulturm'. From this place, the broken terrain was observed. It is said that the tower is as deep as it is high. Its lower part used to be a dungeon where many an unhappy prisoner wasted away and his remains putrefied, hence the name 'Faulturm' since the allusion is to the 'foul' remnants left here.

*Part of the city walls showing the imposing bulk of the Faulturm which served as a lookout between the Röder Gate and Spital ramparts.*

## 2 The Old Forge and the Sentry Walk

From the 'Faulturm' we walk along on the battlements from which we can watch through embrasures courts and roofs full of nooks. We come across the steep gable of the Old Forge, a truly charming old building. The plaques set between the loopholes are in acknowledgement of those who have given money to restore and maintain the town's battlements since the last war. Today, Rothenburg continues to seek those kind people who will help to keep the walls intact by contributing what they can to this end. And, as a recognition of that service, the town then places a plaque on its wall.

We can see by the way the houses snuggle together immediately behind the city walls how much space was at a premium within its protective embrace.

*The Old Forge. In the background the romantic timbered gable, the city wall with its sentry walk and the Röder Gate's tower.*

*Roofed sentry walk and city walls.*

## 3 Das Rödertor (The Röder Gateway)

At the next towergate, the Röder Gateway or Arch, we go downstairs the battlements and walk around the bastion. The sentry walk is reinforced by a so-called 'Zwinger' running parallel. The main gate was further secured in 1615 by a bastion having a double moat, a drawbridge and three gated archways. As with the other gate, the Burgtor, there are two guardrooms and customs houses set in front of the main entrance. The main tower can be climbed and affords a superb view over the town's confusion of roofs and the continuous bustle of the Old Town's lanes.

*Rödertor (Röder Gate) showing its double-moat fortifications, three arches and 'Zwinger' in front of the main gate. In the foreground are the guardrooms and customs houses.*

(i) **Röderturm:**
Times of opening 1st April to 31st October, open daily from 9 a. m. to 6 p. m.

*Mark's Tower and Röderbogen.* ▶

*View from Röder Gate (Rödertor) towards the battlements with their gates and sentry walks.*

## 24 Markusturm (Mark's Tower) and Röderbogen (Röder Arch)

Walking through the 'Rödergasse' into town direction we arrive at Markusturm which, together with Röderbogen, is what is left of the oldest fortifications of the city. Below the steep hip-roof which was added later, we can still quite easily recognize the original course of the crenelated battlement wall that used to form its top. The bailiff's house next to it was used as a prison up to the 18th century, and today houses the city's archives. The Röder Arch (Röderbogen) and the sturdy Markus Tower, the simple Renaissance fountain in the foreground together with the half-timbered houses laced with vine leaves to the right make this one of the most charming views Rothenburg has to offer.

*Markus tower with the Röder arch and the executioner's house.*

If you were not tired yet, you shouldn't forget to turn left in front of the Röder Arch and walk along the old town moat up to the house No. 26. The 'Alt-Rothenburg Handwerkerhaus'.

# 5  Old Rothenburg's Craftsmen's House

It was built between 1270 and 1300 and, during the course of seven centuries, housed tradesmen of various sorts. In order, they were vatmakers, leadback dyers, weavers, shoemakers, tinkers, potters, basket-makers, soap-boilers, pavers, tinfounders and bricklayers.

The preservation of this jewel of a house is owing to a hermit who lived in it for many years right up into modern times, maintaining the house in its original condition since he neither required running water nor electricity. The 38 ft. (14 m) deep well inside the house could supply a household with sufficient water even today. The low ceilings and doorways recall to mind that the people of former centuries were not so tall as we are today. Among the eleven furnished rooms and smaller chambers, probably the kitchen with its open range is the most interesting. The irregularly shaped oven tiles in the living room were produced in the 14th century on a potter's wheel.

*Old Rothenburg's Craftsmen's House (13th cent.) showing journeyman's room and cabin bed.*

*Old Rothenburg's Craftmen's House: The shoemaker's workshop.*

(i) **Old Rothenburg's Craftmen's House:** Alter Stadtgraben 26
Times of opening: 1st April to 31st October, daily from 10 a.m.
to 6 p.m. During the "Wintermärchen" (Winter Fairly Tales) open
daily from 2 p.m. to 4 p.m.

## 26 Weißer Turm (White Tower) and Chapel Square (Kapellenplatz)

The White Tower is one of the few remaining relics of the earliest inner city fortifications and dates back to the 12th century. The adjoining half-timbered building is called the Judentanzhaus (Jew's Dance House) which also served as an inn at one time. From here began the Jewish Quarter where some 500 Jews once lived but who where driven out of the city in 1520. Later, this house was turned into a house to shelter the poor and was called 'Seelhaus' or 'Soul House'. The well in the neighbouring Chapel Square is still referred to as 'Seelbrunnen'.

The square however derives its name from the Chapel of St. Mary (Marienkapelle) which was pulled down between 1804 and 1805 and which up to the end of the 14th century had been the synagogue serving Rothenburg's Jewish community. It was here that the Jews had their quarter before they were moved into the new Jew's Lane (Juden-gasse) outside the inner city wall.

*The White Tower, part of the oldest city fortifications, (12th century). Built on to it to the left, the half-timbered facade of the Jew's Dance Hall.*

*The Würzburg Gate or Gallows Gate (Galgentor) with its anterior gate and adjacent towers, moat and ramparts.*

## 27 Galgentor (Gallows Gate)

This lane once led out of the city to the gallows outside the city walls. The gate was a visible landmark of the city's legal jurisdiction as an imperial city. After the loss of this right in 1810 it was pulled down. Both this gate and the Würzburg Gate were those hardest fought for in trying to gain entry into the city. It was here that Tilly's and Turène's troops marched into the city during the Thirty Years's War. Of the fortifications of that time only the formidable gate tower and one of the front gates remain. The moat, barricade and two further towers have gone.

The Galgentor marks the end each year of the historic march of troops which sets off from Spitaltor on the afternoon of every Whit Monday.

The participants encamp the night before in the fields outside the city, so giving a colourful impression of the life of the soldiery of those times, and in addition to the interest that this pageant affords, a secret underground passage has recently been found and is now open to the public. For children, there is excitement to be found on two new playgrounds, one in the Wallgraben and the other at the Spitaltor.

## 8/9 Double Bridge and the 'Kobolzeller Kirchlein' or 'Little Church'

The 'Double Bridge' (erected 1330) which was once dignified by a defensive tower, served as a further security measure in protecting the Kobolzeller Gate.

From the other side there is ample opportunity to take photographs of the city which might include the bridge and Kobolzeller Little Church in the foreground while above, the city's turreted silhouette forms an excellent background. The late Gothic church dating from the fifteenth century unfortunately ransomed the greater part of its treasures during the Peasants' War. Incited by one Dr. Karlstadt, the "Picture Stormer", Müller, his accomplice, had the church plundered on Easter Monday 1526, destroying the works of art found there and throwing the rest into the river.

*The turreted, fortified medieval town of Rothenburg rising over the Tauber Valley with its arched bridge, built 1330.*

*Topplerschlößchen (Mayor Toppler's Little House) built for him in the Tauber Valley during the 14th century.*

## 30  Toppler's Little Castle – Das Topplerschlösschen

Crossing the Double Bridge, we reach after a short walk an odd, castle-like building, Toppler's Little Castle. It was built for Mayor in

*Topplerschlößchen (Toppler's Little Castle) showing the parlour once belonging to Rothenburg's most distinguished lord mayor.*

1388 and served as his summer house and also as a place where he could hold political talks with important people. According to local tradition, it is said that King Wenzel was often a guest here.

Heinrich Toppler, a most competent lord mayor, even referred to sometimes as the "King of Rothenburg", saw to it that the land outside the town was a safe place to dwell and it is probable that this house, standing as it does outside the city walls, was to demonstrate that feeling of security. The tower, decorated with coats of arms, reminds one strongly of the Romanesque, residential towers which, two hundred years earlier, were quite common. The interior is exactly the same as it was at the time it was lived in and open all the year round to visitors.

Toppler's Little Castle, built in the 14th century for Heinrich Toppler, mayor of Rothenburg.

**(i)**  **Topplerschlößchen:**
Im Taubertal. Times of opening from 1st December to 31st October only Fr./Sa. and Su. from 1 p.m. to 4 p.m. In November closed.

*Detwang, an old village in the Tauber Valley not far from Rothenburg*

## 3| The parish church at Detwang

Half an hour's walk, leaving the town by Klingenturm or along the north-western part of the city walls, will bring us to the hamlet of Detwang. Its parish church of St. Peter and St. Paul was consecrated in the year 968 and belongs to the oldest churches in Franconia. The focal point of this church, however, is probably its altar, again the work of Tilman Riemenschneider. Originally created to be set up in St. Michael's chapel in Rothenburg in 1510, it was taken from that church after having been badly damaged in the Thirty Year's War and taken to Detwang for safekeeping. While the altar wings depicting the scene from the Mount of Olives and that of Christ's resurrection from the dead are the work of one of his assistants, the main group of figures is by the hand of the master himself.

*The Romanesque parish church at Detwang, St. Peter and St. Paul, consecrated in the year 968.*

*The Altar of the Cross in Detwang, another work by Tilman Riemenschneider.*

*The Altar of the Cross – Mary weeping.*

**Detwang Parish Church:**

Open from 1st Jan. to 31st March from 10 a.m. to 12 midday and 2 p.m. to 4 p.m. Closed Mondays. From 1st April to 31st October open from 8.30 a.m. to midday and from 1.30 p.m. to 5 p.m.

## Historical pageants and events

Please see under 'Annual Events'

The 'Meistertrunk' or 'Mighty Draught'

This has been played annually ever since 1881 at Whitsuntide by amateur groups to audiences of ten thousand or more and recently on the second Saturday in July (Festliche Sommertage) and in September (Reichsstadt Festtage).

The play is about the remarkable saving of the town on October 31st, 1631 during the Thirty Years' War. Because of the heavy resistance the town had put against its besiegers, Tilly, general of the invading forces,

*Performance of the historical festival of the "Meistertrunk" in the Kaisersaal of the town hall.*

was furious when he finally took the town and vowed as was customary to hang every man jack of the city council. All appeals to him for mercy were of no avail and the mayor of the city, Bürgermeister Bezold was summoned to fetch the executioner. In the meantime, however, the general was offered an enormous tankard containing three and half of the best Franconian wine (nearly seven pints!). Tilly, on seeing this, thereupon promised to show mercy if one of the councillors could swallow this off in one draught. Former Bürgermeister Nusch accepted the challenge and succeeded in finishing off the wine in one go to the amzement of Tilly who was constrained to keep his promise and so the town's population fell to rejoicing.

*Historical City Festival. General Tilly with his officers.*

*Mayor Nusch, emptying the 3 ¼ litres bumper.*

## The historic Shepherds' Dance

Every year, at Easter and on Whit Sunday, as well as on the second Saturday in July and September, the 'Guild of Shepherds' meets in the afternoon to dance in front of the Town Hall. Even in the Middle Ages, the shepherds held their dance round the Herterichs Well to the south

*The historic "Schäfertanz" (Sheperds' Dance) on the Market Place in front of the Town Hall.*

side of the Town Hall. According to legend, they were able to drive out the plague from Rothenburg with their dancing. Another story goes that one of the shepherds of those times had a wonderful dream in which he found a treasure and the shepherds dance with pleasure as a consequence.

## The Hans-Sachs-Play

Hans Sachs (1494-1576) was a shoemaker by trade and lived in Nuremberg as a 'Meistersinger' at the same time making himself a name as a 'Shoemaker poet'. He wrote numerous verses, among them 208 plays for the theatre. A Rothenburg theatre group has been performing his plays every Easter and Whitsuntide particularly and in the summer months from May to August inclusive since 1921 and especially on the festival days of the imperial city, the Reichsstadt-Festtagen, when some of his finest pieces are performed in the Kaisersaal of the Town Hall. As well as being played against such an impressive historical backdrop, the poignancy of the occaision is strengthened by the costume and music of the 'Meistersinger' period.

*The Hans Sachs Plays here showing a scene from one of the farces taken from the Nuremberg "Cobbler Poets" repertoire being performed in the Imperial Room of the Town Hall.*

### Easter Programme

The Easter festival offers its visitors the historic 'Shepherds' Dance' referred to above, a performance of the Hans Sachs Plays Cycle as well as Easter concerts on the Market Place and an organ concert. The Puppet Theatre for Adults at the Burgtor invites visitors to its performances.

*Whitsuntide (mid-summer) programme showing medieval camp life.*

### Whitsuntide Programme

Amateur players perform the 'Meistertrunk' (The Mighty Draught) once on Saturday afternoon and twice on the following Sunday and Monday of Whit Week in the Kaisersaal of the Town Hall. The Guild of Shepherds perform their dance on Sunday, and, as at Easter, Hans Sachs Plays, the Puppet Theatre for Adults, as well as concerts both in the Jakobskirche and in the open air are offered as additional entertainment. On the Monday of this week the visitor may well feel himself transported in time back to the Thirty Years' War. Already in the early morning, troops march through the town and in the afternoon at about three o'clock, the 'Historic Army 1631' files through the town from Spitaltor via Spitalgasse, Schmiedgasse and Galgengasse towards Gallows Gate (Galgentor) where the participants set up an army encampment.

### The 'Festliche Sommertage' in Rothenburg ob der Tauber

These 'days of summer festival' take place on the second weekend of July to which visitors are cordially invited. There is a citizens' festival which includes a 'Biergarten' on the Town Hall Square which opens on Saturday afternoon and offers separate entertainment during the evening. On Sunday, the 'Meistertrunk' play alluded to above is performed once more together with the Shepherds' Dance in the afternoon.

### Reichsstadt-Festtage (The Imperial City's Festival)

The second weekend in September is once more dedicated to the history of the city. It commences with a torchlight procession of those taking part in the historical festival on Friday evening as they begin their march from the Tauber Valley up into the city and to the Market Place. On the following day in the afternoon, the people of Rothenburg offer their guests scenes from the town's historic past over a period of seven centuries in the streets and lanes of the town and on its squares. In the evening, there is a firework display and illuminations which are to recall the bombardment of the city in former times. On Sunday, the festival goes on throughout the day and once more includes the 'Meistertrunk' performance and the Shepherds' Dance described above.

# Historical pageants and events

# in Rothenburg

# The Lord's Church at Creglingen

Here is to be found what is probably the most perfect work ever wrought by the hand of Riemenschneider, the St. Mary Altar at the Lord's Church (Herrgottskirche) in Creglingen, 17 kms (10½ miles) beyond Detwang.

*The Church of the Lord at Creglingen. The altar of the Virgin Mary, one of Tilman Riemenschneider's masterpieces.*

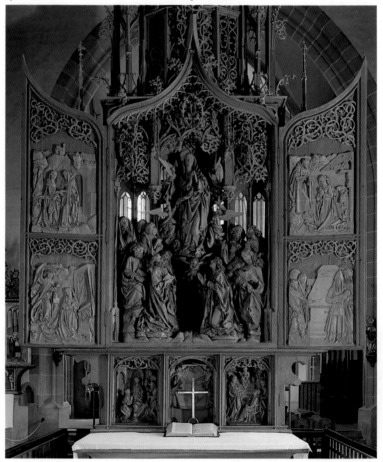

## Winter in Rothenburg

Beginning from December onwards up until New Year's Day, the town is able to offer its guests and visitors a full, interesting programme of events which include those of a reflective character, those of a romantic and historical quality as well as those which are jolly and entertaining. There are Christmas serenades, choir and organ concerts, string music, children's singing and children's theatre, performances by the Rothenburg 'Sternsinger' and Christmas evenings in hotels which have a musical background to them. Here, the friend of music is really spoiled! Added to this, there are also torchlight processions of children, torchlight rambles, hikes through the woods (which also include a stop-by for punch), trips by old stage coach for children as well as guides round the town and its museums. Annual events at this time are the Christmas Crib in the Town Hall, an exhibition of art, the Hans Sachs performances and the Puppet Theatre for Adults as well as the Christmas Market.

*Romantic winter scene around the Town Hall entrance.*

Winter's atmosphere in Rothenburg

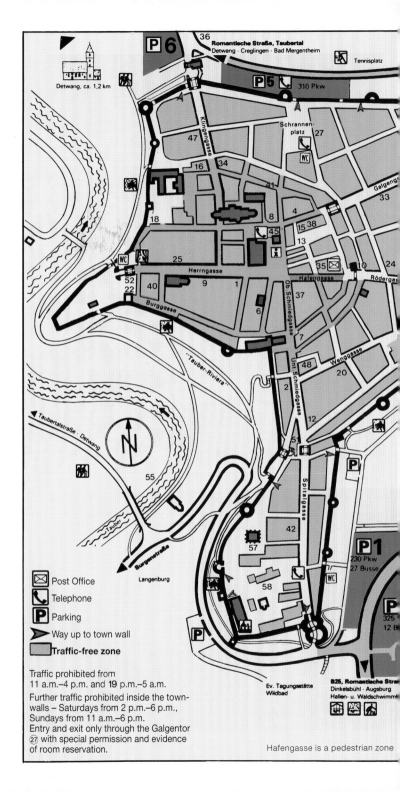

P6

36 **Romantische Straße, Taubertal**
Detwang · Creglingen · Bad Mergentheim

Tennisplatz

Detwang, ca. 1,2 km

P5 310 Pkw

47

Klingengasse

Schrannen-
platz 27

WC

16 34

41

Galgengasse

33

18

8 4

15 38

45

13

25

Herrngasse

35 10 24

Rödergasse

WC

Hafengasse

52

9 1

Ob. Schmiedgasse

37

22

40

6

Burggasse

7

"Tauber-Riviera"

48

Wenggasse

Unt. Schmiedgasse

2

20

12

Taubertalstraße · Detwang

51

N

Spitalgasse

55

P1
230 Pkw
27 Busse

42

57

WC

Burgenstraße

58

P

Langenburg

325
12 Bu

⊠ Post Office

Telephone

P Parking

Way up to town wall

Traffic-free zone

Ev. Tagungsstätte
Wildbad

**B25, Romantiche Stra**
Dinkelsbühl · Augsburg
Hallen- u. Waldschwimm

Traffic prohibited from
11 a.m.–4 p.m. and 19 p.m.–5 a.m.

Further traffic prohibited inside the town-
walls – Saturdays from 2 p.m.–6 p.m.,
Sundays from 11 a.m.–6 p.m.
Entry and exit only through the Galgentor
㉗ with special permission and evidence
of room reservation.

Hafengasse is a pedestrian zone

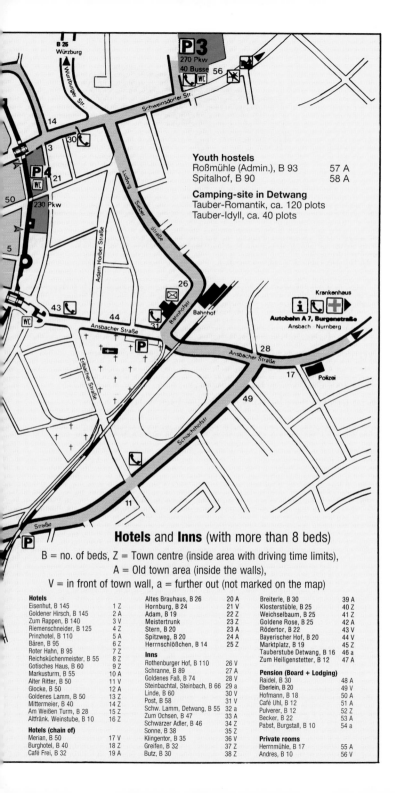

**Youth hostels**
Roßmühle (Admin.), B 93     57 A
Spitalhof, B 90     58 A

**Camping-site in Detwang**
Tauber-Romantik, ca. 120 plots
Tauber-Idyll, ca. 40 plots

## Hotels and Inns (with more than 8 beds)

B = no. of beds, Z = Town centre (inside area with driving time limits),
A = Old town area (inside the walls),
V = in front of town wall, a = further out (not marked on the map)

| Hotels | | |
|---|---|---|
| Eisenhut, B 145 | 1 Z | |
| Goldener Hirsch, B 145 | 2 A | |
| Zum Rappen, B 140 | 3 V | |
| Riemenschneider, B 125 | 4 Z | |
| Prinzhotel, B 110 | 5 A | |
| Bären, B 95 | 6 Z | |
| Roter Hahn, B 95 | 7 Z | |
| Reichsküchenmeister, B 55 | 8 Z | |
| Gotisches Haus, B 60 | 9 Z | |
| Markusturm, B 55 | 10 A | |
| Alter Ritter, B 50 | 11 V | |
| Glocke, B 50 | 12 A | |
| Goldenes Lamm, B 50 | 13 Z | |
| Mittermeier, B 40 | 14 Z | |
| Am Weißen Turm, B 28 | 15 Z | |
| Altfränk. Weinstube, B 10 | 16 Z | |

| Hotels (chain of) | | |
|---|---|---|
| Merian, B 50 | 17 V | |
| Burghotel, B 40 | 18 Z | |
| Café Frei, B 32 | 19 A | |

| | | |
|---|---|---|
| Altes Brauhaus, B 26 | 20 A | |
| Hornburg, B 24 | 21 V | |
| Adam, B 19 | 22 Z | |
| Meistertrunk | 23 Z | |
| Stern, B 20 | 23 A | |
| Spitzweg, B 20 | 24 A | |
| Herrnschlößchen, B 14 | 25 Z | |

| Inns | | |
|---|---|---|
| Rothenburger Hof, B 110 | 26 V | |
| Schranne, B 89 | 27 A | |
| Goldenes Faß, B 74 | 28 V | |
| Steinbachtal, Steinbach, B 66 | 29 a | |
| Linde, B 60 | 30 V | |
| Post, B 58 | 31 V | |
| Schw. Lamm, Detwang, B 55 | 32 a | |
| Zum Ochsen, B 47 | 33 A | |
| Schwarzer Adler, B 46 | 34 Z | |
| Sonne, B 38 | 35 Z | |
| Klingentor, B 35 | 36 V | |
| Greifen, B 32 | 37 Z | |
| Butz, B 30 | 38 Z | |

| | | |
|---|---|---|
| Breiterle, B 30 | 39 A | |
| Klosterstüble, B 25 | 40 Z | |
| Weichselbaum, B 25 | 41 Z | |
| Goldene Rose, B 25 | 42 A | |
| Rödertor, B 22 | 43 V | |
| Bayerischer Hof, B 20 | 44 V | |
| Marktplatz, B 19 | 45 Z | |
| Tauberstube Detwang, B 16 | 46 a | |
| Zum Heiligenstetter, B 12 | 47 A | |

| Pension (Board + Lodging) | | |
|---|---|---|
| Raidel, B 30 | 48 A | |
| Eberlein, B 20 | 49 V | |
| Hofmann, B 18 | 50 A | |
| Café Uhl, B 12 | 51 A | |
| Pulverer, B 12 | 52 Z | |
| Becker, B 22 | 53 A | |
| Pabst, Burgstall, B 10 | 54 a | |

| Private rooms | | |
|---|---|---|
| Herrnmühle, B 17 | 55 A | |
| Andres, B 10 | 56 V | |

Castle Gardens (five minutes' walk from the Town Hall; lighted after dark)

Castle Gardens – Tauber Valley – Kobolzell Church – Double Bridge – Kobolzell Gate

Castle Gardens – Toppler Castle – Fuchs Mill – Steg Mill – footpath leading to the Prison Tower

Toppler Castle – Engelsburg Klosterweg – Tauber Valley – Detwang

Marked circuits (about two hours) starting from the town:

Magpie:
Hospital Gate – Schandtaubertal – (Schandtauber Valley) – Blinktal (Blink Valley) – Kobolzeller Tor – (Kobolzeller Gate)

Milan:
Hospital Gate – Dove Valley – Natursteig – Hospital Gate

Fox:
Kobolzeller Gate – Double Bridge – Engelsburg (Angel's Stronghold) – Klingentor

Wagtail:
Gallows Gate – Steffeleins Well – Steinbachtal – (Stoneditch Valley) – Klingentor

Hare:
Gallows Gate – Steffeleins Well – Steinsbachtal – Bettwar – Klingentor

# Index

# Practical hints from A–Z

**Police** (accident, robbery etc.): Tel. 110
**Fire:** Tel. 112
**First Aid Ambulance** (Bavarian Red Cross),
Tel. 19222

**Aerodrome** (flights over city): Aero-Club,
Bauerngruben, Tel. 7474

**Camping:** camping place at Tauberidyll, Detwang,
Tel. 3177, and Tauberromantik, Detwang, Tel. 6191

**Changing money:** Possible at all banks and at the
Tourist Office (Reisebüro) am Marktplatz.
Also at Hotel Tilman Riemenschneider,
Georgengasse 11–13

**Children's playgrounds:** special playgrounds for
adventure in the 'Wallgräben' am Würzburger Tor
(Würzburger Gate) and am Spital Tor. Others at
the indoor swimming pool and Nördlinger Straße

**Church services:** Catholic – Sundays, 7 a.m.,
8.30 a.m. and 10.30 a.m. held in the Church of
St. John (Johanniskirche). Protestant – Sundays,
7 a.m. and 9 a.m. in the St. Jakobskirche.

**Fishing:** District Fishing Association (Bezirks-
Fischereiverein) and on 3289 (to Mr. Schmid)

**General Information:** Rooms and accommodation,
local events and tourist assistance etc. D-8803
Rothenburg ob der Tauber, Marktplatz 2
(Ratstrinkstube), Tel. 0 90 61-404-92,
Postfach 1114, Telex 61 379 roti d, Fax 86 207

**Golf:** Golf course: Schloß Colmberg, 18 kms
(approx. 11 miles), Tel. 0 98 03-2 62

**Group arrangements:** Guided tours round the city
both day and night. Reception by the city's 'master
sutler', visit by the town's traditional nightwatch-
man, walks over Engelsburg (Angel's Hill) to Detwang, guided tour; special performances of Hans
Sachs' Puppet Theatre, dance music with Hans
Sachs and his music, and organ recitals. All information about this and other details from the Verkehrsamt (Tourist Office), for address please see
above under 'General Information'.

**Guided tours:** May to October and December daily
at 11 a.m. and 2 p.m. April daily at 2 p.m. Minimum
number of 10 persons per group.

**Kneipp water treading:** Am Schaupfad 'Riviera'.

**Lending Library** and Reading Room; Klingengasse 6, Tel. 20 11 (closed Wednesdays)

**Lost property:** Rathaus-Arkaden (Town Hall
Arcade) entrance far left; Tel. 404-56

**Museums:** Imperial City Museum, crime museum
furnished as in the Middle Ages, Alt Rothenburger

Handwerkshaus (Old Rothenburg's Tradesmen's
House), Topplerschlößchen, 'Historiengewölbe',
Puppenmuseum (Doll Museum). For times of
opening see information accompanying relevant
text.

**Old-time coach trips:** Tours of the town as
well as half-day and full-day excursions. Further
information obtainable at the Verkehrsamt.

**Places to sit and relax:** Walks round the Old Town,
in Burggarten and along the Tauber 'Riviera'

**Post offices:** Milchmarkt 5, Bahnhofstraße 7,
Rückertstraße 4

**Railways** (Bundesbahn): Information at the railway station (Bahnhof), Tel. 19419

**Rambling and Hiking:** A marked path for ramblers
through the Tauber Valley over the Engelburg
heights (which gives one a Merian Panorama over
the valley and town) and also in the wooded area of
Frankenhöhe. For tickets, see pp. 79–80 and also at
the 'Verkehrsamt'.

**Reichsstadthalle:** Großer Saal (Main hall) seats 600
persons, also smaller room and parking facilities;
Spitalhof, Tel. 4866

**Rent-a-cycle:** Railway station (Bahnhof),
Rothenburg, Tel. 23 30.

**Riding:** Reitstall am Schwanensee 3 kms away
(approx 2 miles). Tel. 32 62

**Sauna:** See below.

**Small arms club:** air guns, pistols and rifles. Open
to guests on Thursdays between 8 and 10 p.m.
Schützengilde (Small Arms Club), Paul-Finkler-
Straße, Tel. 32 77

**Swimming and Sauna:** Ozone indoor swimming
pool (mid September to mid May) and heated out-
door swimming pool (mid May to mid September),
Tel. 45 65. Sauna and massage: Tel. 56 66;
Restaurant with large terrace, Tel. 39 71,
Nördlinger Straße (The Romantic Route)

**Telephoning:** Local dialling code: 09861 (From abroad, omit '0'. Directory Enquiries (inland): 0118;
Directory Enquiries (abroad): 00118; Sending tele-
grams: 01131; Kiosks: please see city plan, pages
77–78

**Travel agency:** Marktplatz 2 (Ratstrinkstube),
Tel. 46 11.

**Youth hostels:** Roßmühle, Mühlacker 1, Tel. 9 41 60;
Spitalhof, Tel. 78 89; Jugendzentrum, Klingengasse 6, Tel. 13 33